peace

wendy anderson halperin

ATHENEUM BOOKS FOR YOUNG READERS

New York   London   Toronto   Sydney   New Delhi

$\mathcal{A}$
atheneum

ATHENEUM BOOKS FOR YOUNG READERS

An imprint of Simon & Schuster Children's Publishing Division

1230 Avenue of the Americas, New York, New York 10020

Copyright © 2013 by Wendy Anderson Halperin

For information about special discounts for bulk purchases, please contact Simon & Schuster
Special Sales at 1-866-506-1949 or business@simonandschuster.com.

The Simon & Schuster Speakers Bureau can bring authors to your live event. For more information or to
book an event, contact the Simon & Schuster Speakers Bureau at 1-866-248-3049 or visit our website at
www.simonspeakers.com.

Book design by Sonia Chaghatzbanian

The text for this book is set in Love Ya Like A Sister.

The illustrations for this book are rendered in watercolor and pencils.

Manufactured in China

1112 SCP

First Edition

10 9 8 7 6 5 4 3 2 1

CIP data for this book is available from the Library of Congress

ISBN 978-0-689-82552-1

ISBN 978-1-4424-6787-3 (eBook)

dedicated to your senses

To Seeing

May your eyes have visions of peace. May your eyes see actions of peace. May you find peace in seeing the wonders of nature.

To Touching

May your hands do the work of peace: to help, to plant, to comfort, to reach out, and to create peace. May your feet walk in the direction of peace.

To Smelling

May you smell fresh air. May you smell a twig of rosemary when you are upset. May you smell the flowers of a quiet garden and the trees in a silent woods, and may a flower teach you to breathe slowly and deeply.

To Tasting

May you make choices in what you eat to promote peace. May your thoughts and efforts help feed the hungry. May you help keep our waters, lakes, rivers, and oceans clean for the thirsty.

To Hearing

May you hear or make music to feel peace. May you be a good listener to promote peace. May your words heal, not hurt.

With special thanks to Ruta Rimas; Sonia Chaghatzbanian; Kaitlin Severini; Coleman McCarthy; Rubin Pfeffer; R. Carlos Nakai; Leslie Zillman; my family: John, Kale, Joel, Lane; and my parents, Haas, and Andy. Thank you all for helping me find PEACE.

—W. A. H.

For there to be
peace in the world . . .

... there must be

"what you do not want done to you, do not do to others." —CONFUCIUS

"How do we put ourselves in other people's shoes and really feel what

peace in nations.

"Anger dwells only in the bosom of fools." —ALBERT EINSTEIN

they feel and then use that information to fuel solutions?" — PAUL BENNETT

"If a person really knows what goes around comes around they wouldn't commit evil acts." —MAYA ANGELOU

those we encounter and those around us, along the way." —JEREMY ALDANA

"See no evil, hear no evil, speak no evil." —JAPANESE PROVERB

"Teach Peace." —BUMPER STICKER

there must be peace in cities.

"Everything has its beauty, but not everyone sees it." —CONFUCIUS

greed. If people all over the world . . . would do this, it would change the earth." —WILLIAM FAULKNER

"Too often we underestimate the power of a touch, a smile, a kind word, a listening ear, an honest compliment,

"A man is but the product of his thoughts.

For there to be peace in cities,

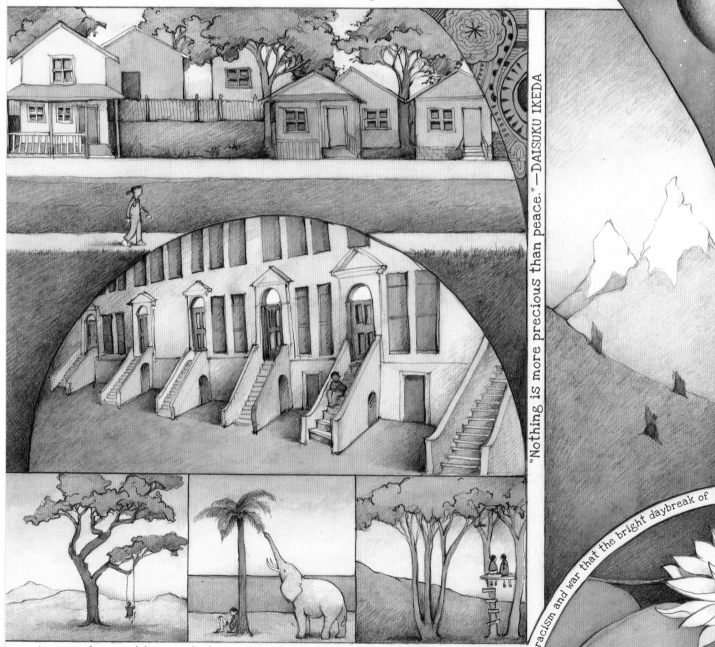

"Nothing is more precious than peace." —DAISUKU IKEDA

racism and war that the bright daybreak of

"I refuse to accept the view that mankind is so tragically bound to the starless midnight of

or the simple act of caring, all of which have the potential to turn a life around." —LEO F. BUSCAGLIA

what he thinks, he becomes." —GANDHI

there must be peace in neighborhoods.

"Seek to build not destroy." —NEALE DONALD WALSCH

"There is no way to peace; peace is the way." —A. J. MUSTE

peace and brotherhood can never become a reality.

". . . Unarmed truth and unconditional love will have the final word. . . ." —MARTIN LUTHER KING JR.

"Friendship is the only cure for hatred, the only guarantee of peace."—BUDDHA

"Great compassion makes a peaceful heart."—MAHA GHOSANANDA

"One of the secrets of inner peace is the practice of compassion."—DALAI LAMA

For there to be peace in neighborhoods,

"It is the law of love that rules mankind."—GANDHI

"Peace is always beautiful."—WALT WHITMAN

"Education is the most powerful weapon which you

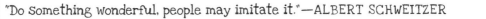

"Do something wonderful, people may imitate it."—ALBERT SCHWEITZER

"Our life is shaped by our mind."—BUDDHA

"There is no trust more sacred than the one the world holds with children."—KOFI A. ANNAN

there must be peace in schools.

"To reach peace, teach peace."—POPE JOHN PAUL II

"Compassion is the chief law of human existence."—FYODOR DOSTOYEVSKY

can use to change the world."—NELSON MANDELA

"When we give cheerfully and accept gratefully, everyone is blessed." —MAYA ANGELOU

"All works of love are works of peace." —MOTHER TERESA

"The great gift of human beings is that we have the power of empathy." —MERYL STREEP

"He has a right to criticize who has the heart to help." —ABRAHAM LINCOLN

"This is the way of peace: Overcome evil with good, and falsehood with truth, and hatred with love." —PEACE PILGRIM

For there to be peace in schools,

"If in our daily life we can smile, if we can be peaceful and happy, not only we, but everyone

"Once forgiving begins, dreams can be rebuilt." —BEVERLY FLANIGAN

"Peace is the only battle worth waging." —ALBERT CAMUS

"Without forgiveness, without reconciliation, we have no future." —DESMOND TUTU

"An eye for an eye makes the whole world blind." —GANDHI

"Forgiveness is the fragrance the violet sheds on the heel that has crushed it." —MARK TWAIN

there must be peace in homes.

will profit from it. This is the most basic kind of peace work." —THICH NHAT HANH

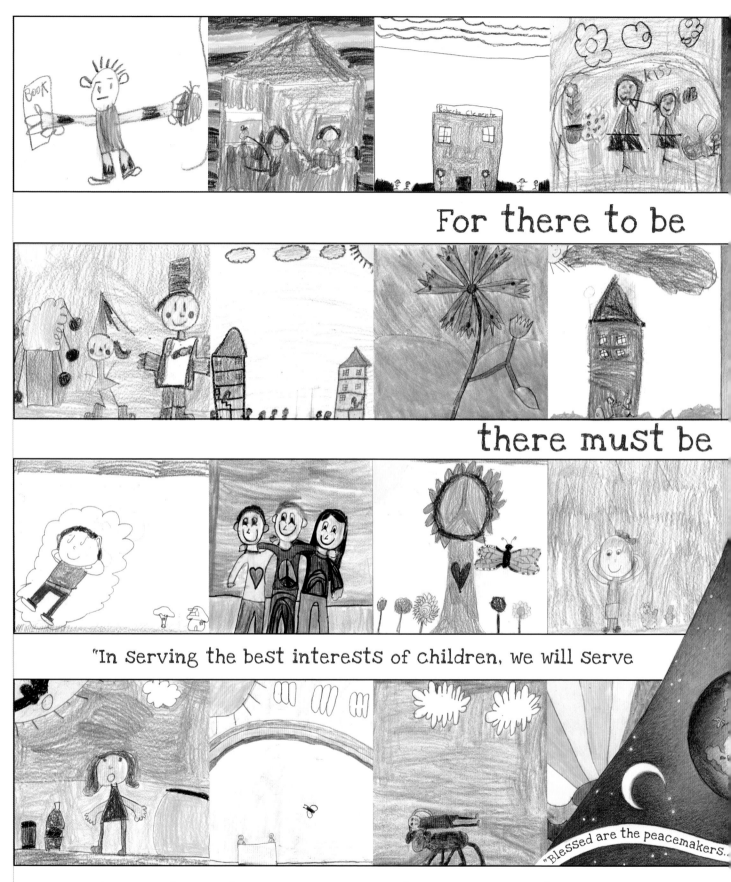

For there to be

there must be

"In serving the best interests of children, we will serve

"Blessed are the peacemakers."

"Peace. It does not mean to be in a place where there is no noise, trouble, or hard work.

peace in homes,

peace in our hearts.

the best interests of all humanity." —CAROL BELLAMY

—THE NEW TESTAMENT

It means to be in the midst of those things and still be calm in your heart." —UNKNOWN

"Do your little bit of good where you are; it's those little bits of good put together that overwhelm the world."—DESMOND TUTU

When there is peace in our hearts,

"Good actions give strength to ourselves and inspire good actions in others."—PLATO

"Be the change you want to see in the world."—GANDHI

"Any time you have an opportunity to make a difference in this world and you don't,

"If a person seems wicked, do not cast him away. Awaken him   with your words, elevate him

"When our children are happy, then we are better human beings."—WHOOPI GOLDBERG

"Peace is not something you wish for; it's something you make,

There will be peace in our homes

"what can you do to promote world peace? Go home and love your family."—MOTHER TERESA

"When in doubt, tell the truth."—MARK TWAIN

"A peace above all earthly dignities, a still and quiet conscience."—WILLIAM SHAKESPEARE

just let ourselves feel peace. Peace of mind gives us the strength to keep trying."—ROBERT ALAN SILVERSTEIN

"If I can help an elderly person today, that will help me live more fully."—RIGOBERTA MENCHÚ TUM

"Something you do, something you are, and it's something you give away."—ROBERT FULGHUM

when there is peace in our schools.

"No one has yet fully realized the wealth of sympathy, kindness, and generosity hidden in the soul of a child."—EMMA GOLDMAN

"The object of the superior man is truth."—CONFUCIUS

"Doing nothing for others is the undoing of ourselves."—HORACE MANN

"When we genuinely forgive, we set a prisoner free and then discover that the prisoner we set free was us." —LEWIS B. SMEDES

"I like to listen. I have learned a great deal from listening carefully." —ERNEST HEMINGWAY

"Courage is what it takes to stand up and speak.

Courage is also what it takes to sit down and listen." —WINSTON CHURCHILL

"Darkness cannot drive out darkness: Only light can do that. Hate

There will be peace in our schools

"Today more than ever before, life must be characterized by a sense of universal responsibility,

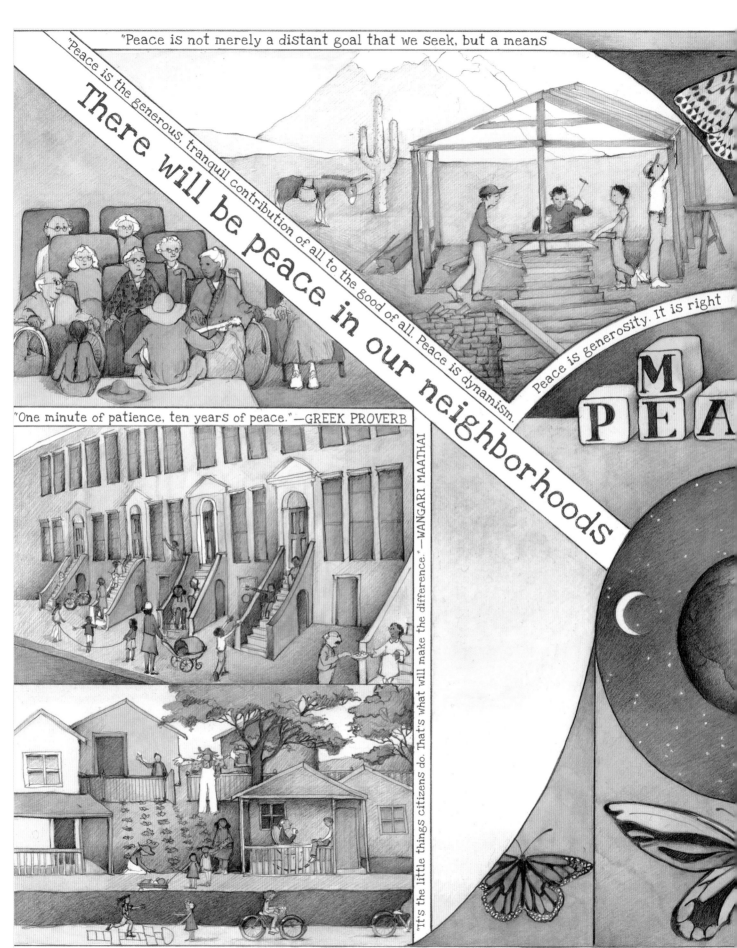

"Peace is not merely a distant goal that we seek, but a means

"Peace is the generous, tranquil contribution of all to the good of all. Peace is dynamism.

There will be peace in our neighborhoods

Peace is generosity. It is right

"One minute of patience, ten years of peace." —GREEK PROVERB

"It's the little things citizens do. That's what will make the difference." —WANGARI MAATHAI

"Peace can be made in the neighborhoods, the living rooms, the playing fields, and in the classrooms of our country

by which we arrive at that goal." —DR. MARTIN LUTHER KING JR.

"You have everything you need for complete peace and total happiness right now." —WAYNE W. DYER

...and it is duty." —ARCHBISHOP ÓSCAR ROMERO

when there is peace in our cities.

"Forgiveness means letting go of the past." —GERALD G. JAMPOLSKY

"We cannot sow seeds with clenched fists." —ADOLFO PÉREZ ESQUIVEL

You still make the personal choices . . . and you are still in charge of your own destiny." —JIMMY CARTER

"Peace is a daily, a weekly, a monthly process, gradually changing opinions, slowly eroding old barriers, quietly building new structures." —JOHN F. KENNEDY

There will be peace in our cities

"Celebrate diversity, practice acceptance, and may we all choose peaceful options to conflict." —DONZELLA MICHELE MALONE

"When people talk, listen completely." —ERNEST HEMINGWAY

"Peace is present only to be awake, alive in the present moment." we need whether or not we are in touch with it. serenity. The ques

"A quiet conscience makes one strong!" —ANNE FRANK

M
W
PEACE

"We are each walking agents of the vision of peace we carry inside us." —KATHLEEN VANDE KIEFT

"The more peace there is in us, the more peace there will also be in our troubled world." —ETTY HILLESUM

when there is peace in our nations.

"Truth is a deep kindness that teaches us to be content in our everyday life." —KAHLIL GIBRAN

right here and now,

in ourselves and in everything we do and see. Every breath we take, every step we make, can be filled with

peace, joy, and

—THICH NHAT HANH

"Peace on earth, good-will to men." —HENRY WADSWORTH LONGFELLOW

"Happiness is part of who we are. Joy is the feeling." —TONY DeLISO

"When the power of love overcomes the love of power, the world will know peace." —JIMI HENDRIX

There will be peace

"When we feel love and kindness toward others, it not only makes others feel loved and cared for,

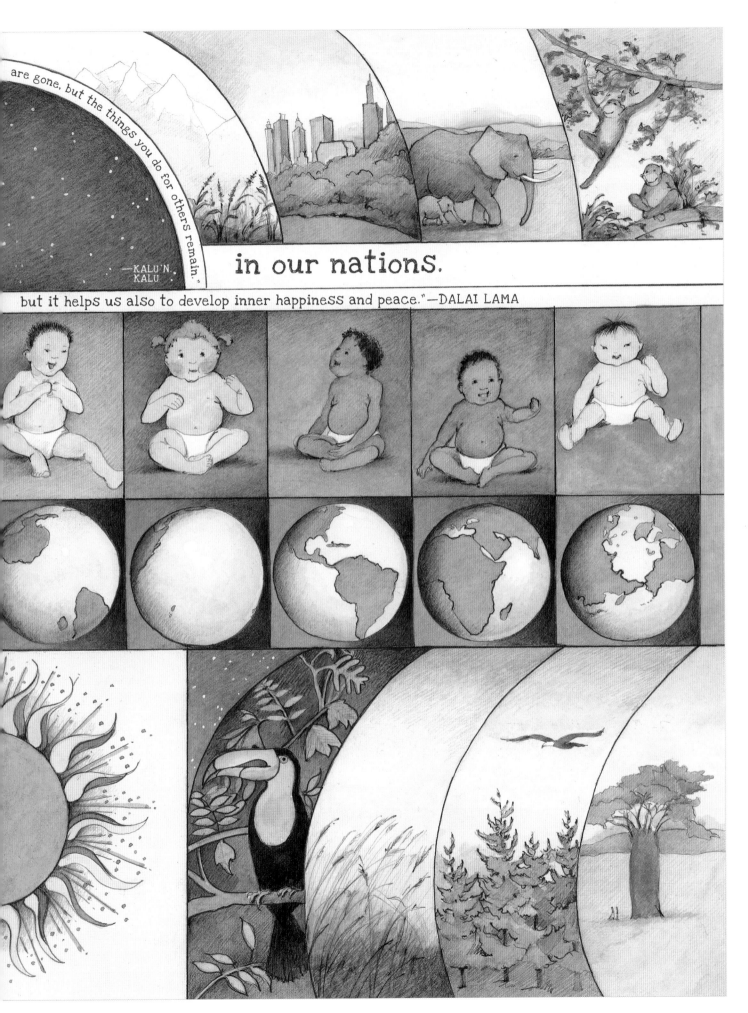

are gone, but the things you do for others remain." —KALU'N KALU

in our nations.

but it helps us also to develop inner happiness and peace." —DALAI LAMA

And we will have

"May the sun bring you new energy by day, may the moon softly restore you by night, may the rain wash away your worries, may the

peace in our world.

breeze blow new strength into your being, may you walk gently through the world and know its beauty all the days of your life." —APACHE BLESSING

acknowledgments

Many special thank-yous to the young artists whose creations
so beautifully and peacefully grace this book:

Maple Grove School (South Haven, MI):
Torry Burrows, Ashleigh Deja, Shayler Trowbridge

Woodbridge Elementary (Zeeland, MI):
Max Jakubowski

Roberto Clemente Learning Academy (Detroit, MI):
Adrian Cantu, Omar Gomez, Yesenia Hernandez, Elida Morales,
Joslyn Licona-Peña, Jonathan Peters, Osiel Segundo-Garcia

Mount Clemens Montessori Academy (Mount Clemens, MI):
Ava Patyi, Benjamin Brooks, Danielle Webster, Jackson Taylor,
Olivia Kozlowski, Caitlyn Moore, Somer Perri

North Shore Elementary School (South Haven, MI):
Sierra Garber, Emily Grooms, Olivia Jones, Sydnee Smith

Saint Mary's School (Saint Clairsville, OH):
Will Balgo, Sean Bushlow, Maggie Marody, Gavin Shields,

Greenwood Elementary (Saint Clair Shores, MI):
Angela Morisette, Isabella Elsey, Karly Thomas

Claremont Elementary (Ossining, NY):
Joseph Chambers